YOUR ASSERTIVE LIFE SERIES

YOUR **ASSERTIVE** LIFE

YOUR ASSERTIVE LIFE SERIES

YOUR **ASSERTIVE** LIFE

How To Become More Assertive, Set Clear Boundaries, and Claim Control of Yourself and Your Life.

Written By:
Andy Raingold

Graphic Design By: Stephen Hawkins.
Special Thanks to Nathanial Dasco & Ikhide Oshoma

Your Assertive Life Series Copyright 2020 ThinkeLife

All Rights Reserved.
No part of this book may be reproduced in any form or by any electronic or mechanical means including information storage and retrieval means without permission in writing from the author.

The only exception is by a reviewer, who may quote short excerpts in a review.

Andy Raingold - ThinkeLife
Visit my website at **www.andyraingold.com**

First printing: Sept 2020.

ISBN: 978 1 913929 87 9

Table of Contents

INTRODUCTION 3
- *What exactly is assertiveness?* 5
- *Assertiver Communication* 6

BOUNDARIES 10
- *The Importance Of Boundaries* 10
- EFFECTS OF NOT HAVING BOUNDARIES 12
  - *Doormat Syndrome* 12
  - *Becoming downtrodden or depressed* 14
  - *Do you share your problems?* 16
  - *Taking on the boss* 17
  - *Get your relationships in order* 18
  - *Write your own rules* 19
  - *Set up penalties* 20
  - *Always try and work together* 20

EVERYDAY ASSERTIVENESS 21
  1. *Practice self-talk* 21
  2. *Seek out conflict* 22
- BEING ASSERTIVE FOR WOMEN 22
- BEING ASSERTIVE FOR MEN 23
- SIMPLE STEPS TO BE MORE ASSERTIVE 23
  1. *Say no to 1/3 of all requests made of you* 24
  2. *Deal with your biggest problem person* 24
  3. *Do what you want a few times a week* 24
- ASSERTIVENESS AND SELF-ESTEEM 24

ASSERTIVENESS 28

WHAT'S STOPPING YOU FROM BECOMING ASSERTIVE? 30

ASSERTIVENESS IN THE WORK PLACE: 40

ASSERTIVENESS AT HOME: 49

- **TEACH YOUR CHILDREN TO BE ASSERTIVE:** 56
- **ASSERTIVENESS TRAINING FOR THE NON-ASSERTIVE** 64
- **HOW TO ASSERTIVELY ASK FOR A RAISE** 76
- **QUESTIONS AND ANSWERS** 79
- **OTHER BOOKS BY ANDY RAINGOLD** 83
- **FREE BOOKS** 85

Introduction

Are you guilty of making excuses instead of asserting yourself and taking positive action to actually change your life?

Do you feel guilty when you tell someone "no"? There's no need to feel guilty once you learn the secrets to saying "no" and meaning it.

Do you find yourself being caught up in arguments you'd rather avoid? You'll never again be caught in that predicament once you learn what to say to avoid the fights.

With this little book, you will come to realize that you can leave an impact on everyone you meet. It is an essential ingredient in the search for a more assertive you.

Consider the many possibilities! You can become a leader of your family and be a respected figure at work.

You're just one step away from total control of your life! Starting right now you can claim the power to boost your relationships, career, and personal life. So, if you want to control your destiny, don't wait another moment to start being an assertive, decision-oriented person.

Here's to a great new future for you and your whole family. We have all been in a position in our life when we should have put up some boundaries but we didn't and so suffered as a consequence.

Starting today, you can finally begin to attain complete control and freedom of yourself and your life! And get what you want in the easiest and nicest way possible!

Here you will discover the secrets of how to easily get your way in relationships and at work, effectively influence others by expressing your opinions and ideas suavely, and cleverly deny others' requests or commands without offending them, all while remaining to be an overall respected and well-liked person!

Take a moment to reflect on how people are treating you...

- Do they treat you like a spineless coward or a five-year old child?
- Do your friends always choose what is "best" for you?
- Does your spouse always call the shots at home?
- Do you have a say in making important decisions?
- Does your boss overload you with more work than you can handle?

If people around you have been manipulating and controlling you so often that you can't stand the abuses any longer, or may not even realize your being controlled or manipulated at all - it's time for you to take some action!

There's no need to suffer endlessly in the prison cell of other people's decisions and commands. You have your own free will to do whatever you want, whenever you please. No one can make you do things against your will!

So, if you are getting too little of what you want and too much of what you do not like, now is the time to assert yourself and claim back complete control of your destiny!

Stop drifting along with no plans and idea of where you will go from here. Stop staying in the comfort zone for too long that you feel uncomfortable facing new challenges.

Now, before you proceed, picture yourself...

- Oozing with self-confidence and being positive about your future.

- Feeling secure in a truthful and stable relationship.
- Gaining the trust and respect of your co-workers and friends.
- Feeling more in command and confident of your own decision making ability.
- Getting the best opportunities to enjoy what you really want from life.

Does that feel good?

People who have learned the ways of assertiveness are enjoying that kind of life every day.

What exactly is assertiveness?

Assertiveness is the ability to express yourself and your rights clearly without necessarily violating anyone else's rights. That means you get to have your way, without offending anyone else.

Assertiveness will help you get just about everything that you really want in life. Assertiveness requires direct, open, and honest communication between people. This can be between you and an associate, a friend, or spouse.

This kind of open communication will make everyone feel better about themselves and each other. More importantly, it will help develop and maintain healthy relationships with friends, loved ones, and co-workers.

Did you know that ONE POWERFUL WORD could save your life?

Part of being assertive is learning how to say this single powerful word. For sure, being assertive will:

- Improve your relationships.
- Move your career forward.

- Earn you the respect of everyone in your life - including your spouse, friends, family, co-workers, even your boss.
- Improve your health by reducing stress hormones like adrenaline.

Now, you might be asking yourself: *"Is it too late for me to become assertive? How do I change for the better?"*

To answer your question, it is never too late to be more assertive. The answer to all of your assertiveness questions lies within this book. It is your ultimate solution if you are tired of being described as indecisive, wishy-washy, and sitting on the fence.

Assertive Communication

Assertiveness is an important communication skill that aims to establish healthy and lasting relationships. An assertive person speaks his own mind to influence others while being respectful of others. So you can push aside all those self-doubts. Learn how to improve your relationships, impress your boss, and even fast track your career.

Don't let others dictate anything you don't like or want to do. By applying the contents of this book you will learn how to get your own way while at the same time earning the respect as well as admiration of everyone you come into contact with.

It is time to get in the game, right now, today! But first, lets take a brief look at what's in store for you:

- How to develop healthy relationships.
- The huge difference between assertiveness and aggressiveness.
- The universal fear of the majority of people.
- Why certain behavioral patterns will not work for you.

- How to say "No" nicely to your boss who keeps on delegating his own project to you.
- Why people continue to say "yes" when they want to say "no"?
- Why being the "go-to" person can be disastrous to your health and career.
- How to stop feeling guilty for saying "no".
- How to apply assertiveness in scenarios involving confrontations.
- The significance of a boundary line.
- How to ensure that your rights are protected.
- How to get your spouse to treat you with consideration and respect.
- One of the biggest roadblocks to asserting yourself.
- How to teach your children to be assertive.
- Assertiveness training for the non-assertive.
- How to effectively boost your self-confidence.
- How to fully eliminate negative self-talk.
- How to speak the assertive language.
- How to apply assertiveness in the area of conflicts and problem solving.
- How to be assertive in a meeting or interview, and get the recognition you deserve.
- How saying "yes" all the time could lead you to an early grave.
- Vital steps you must follow to successfully resolve a conflict with another co-worker.
- The biggest obstacle to your child's personality development.
- How to apply assertiveness to counter negative people.
- How to adjust your behavior to get what you really want.
- How to cure "the disease to please".
- How to earn respect for your actions and decisions.
- How to teach people how to treat you.

- How to develop your children in becoming good listeners, excellent conversationalists, and self-confident, assertive individuals.
- How to assertively ask for a raise.

And a lot, lot more!

So, if you have wondered if it is possible to change your attitude and your behavior, and become an assertive person, then wonder no longer. This is the book for you.

You are just one step away from changing your entire life for the better! Start right at this moment! Decide to become more assertive, decisive, and be more in control of your life. This whole book is about ACTING positively for yourself and in your own best interests. This is not selfish. In fact, it is the most positive thing you could do for yourself and others.

You will influence everyone around you and change your life for the better as well as theirs. Your family, your friends, spouse, co-workers, even your boss will notice the difference in your behavior and attitude.

Make a lasting impression on everyone you meet! No more indecisiveness, no more allowing others to lead you around. Be in charge of your own life! Follow the easy systematic instructions, put those tips to work for you, and imagine the possibilities.

Start now and begin to make your dreams a reality by showing the world the Assertive New You!

It's about time you get your way while earning the respect and admiration of everyone.

Andy Raingold

PART 1:
Boundaries & Everyday Assertiveness

Chapter One

Boundaries

The Importance Of Boundaries

We have all been in a position in our life when we should have put up some boundaries but we didn't and because we failed to do so, we suffered the consequences. Boundaries are one of the most important aspects of your life if you are looking to improve yourself as a person and command respect in every type of environment. But what exactly are boundaries? It can be difficult to define since the term has been thrown around loosely for such a long time, but in this short book we will delve into what exactly boundaries are and why they are important.

There are many types of boundaries depending on the type of situation you may find yourself in. But currently, the dictionary definition of a boundary is this:

"A line which marks the limits of an area; a dividing line" - Oxford Languages

When it comes to personal boundaries we are talking about an inner line, rather than a physical line. Boundaries, from a psychological perspective, therefore refer to things that you are willing to accept or tolerate, those being within your boundaries, and the things that you will not tolerate or accept are outside of your personal boundaries.

People put up different boundaries for different types of people depending on their perception of those people. For example, a father may have a very loose boundary towards his daughter, allowing her to speak to him informally, call him daddy and spill orange juice on his shirt continuously. However, the same man may have a completely different set of boundaries towards people he is an authority over at his workplace. While he would tolerate his daughter not really listening to him when he is trying to explain something to her, it is far less likely that he would do so while at the workplace.

Boundaries therefore in their nature are fluid in the sense that they are person dependant but strict when it comes to their implementation. Boundaries are also the primary way in which people express self-respect. Self-respect as a concept is the ability to realize your own worth, abilities, and value. A lot of people struggle with realizing that they have all of these things and therefore do not set up the proper boundaries, this is something we will go into more detail about later, and because of it, they suffer. But self-respect is something that all human beings should have, but if you find that your self-respect is insufficient then there are ways in which you can obtain more of it.

The reason self-respect and boundaries are intertwined is that setting up a boundary in a particular situation or towards a specific person is almost always an expression of self-respect. Here is a possible example: Imagine for a minute a spouse, it could be a man or a woman. Their partner becomes verbally abusive whenever they drink alcohol and it has been going on for years. The first partner has tolerated it over the years and just absorbed the abuse.

However, one day they had enough of the emotional pain that the abuse was causing and told their partner that they would no longer tolerate the abuse. Either it would stop, the drinking would stop or the consequence would be that they will leave.

The second spouse in this scenario is presenting their boundary as an ultimatum, either you do this or I will do that. And the strictness of that ultimatum is the line that was mentioned earlier, the intrinsic boundary that has been erected. And by putting up that boundary he or she has expressed the fact that they believe that they are worth much more than what they were receiving, they were expressing self-respect.

However, some of you may have deduced that the second spouse may have not been expressing self-respect but rather was acting from the fear that the abuse may have turned into something worse. And this deduction leads to the second role that boundaries play for people: self-preservation. Just like how countries set up fences or border guards at their borders to keep their population safe, intrinsic boundaries are often useful in order to protect oneself emotionally and/or physically. In the example above the boundary acted as a way of preventing further deterioration when it came to the abusive behavior. But many people put up other types of internal boundaries to protect themselves. For example, a son may stop speaking to his father after the latter repeatedly lied to him. By deciding to break off contact with his father the son is putting up a boundary to protect himself from further disappointment.

So that, in essence, is the boundary, it is a way to express either self-respect or to protect oneself. They are important because they help us to show our worth to others and to ensure that we remain safe while we navigate this sometimes difficult world.

Effects Of Not Having Boundaries

We have already touched upon the possible bad effects of not having the proper boundaries, but they need to be extrapolated much further to truly understand the repercussions of not having proper boundaries. We will explore these one by one.

1. Doormat Syndrome

The terms were coined by author Lynne Namka and refer to a person who is constantly letting other people take advantage of them. This could be emotionally, physically or even financially. The doormat is an analogy which refers to being walked all over by other people, or even having them wipe their feet on you. The point of the doormat analogy is the fact that it symbolizes massive amounts of disrespect, both from the person suffering from the syndrome, as well as the people who are exploiting it.

Some people may not even realize that they are suffering from doormat syndrome. They may believe that it is just a part of their personality and does not need to change. These are usually the people who are constantly giving to other people without ever receiving anything in return and believe it to be altruistic. While certainly, you should not be doing kind acts to expect the same in return, there does come a tipping point where the acts you do for other people may be causing more harm than they do good. They are usually a sign of co-dependence, again by both parties involved. When one person constantly gives, in any of the ways mentioned above, another party gets used to constantly receiving and it creates an unhealthy balance where neither one of the parties involved is ultimately happy.

In order to fully deal with doormat syndrome, you have to first realize that you are suffering from it. Ask yourself the following questions to be sure:

a) Are there any areas in my life where I feel like I am constantly giving but I am not receiving anything at all in return? (this could be at work, in your marriage, at school etc.)
b) Do I let other people assert their opinions over mine constantly or do I regularly stand up for what I believe in?
c) Do I constantly feel burnt out from trying to make other people, not myself happy?

The last one is a key point that we have not yet discussed when it comes to doormat syndrome, making other people's happiness your primary priority. While people's happiness should be a priority to people to a certain extent it is dangerous to believe that you are responsible for their happiness in general. Usually, when someone decides they are going to try and make everyone around them happy, they are doing it because they hope someone would try in turn to make them happy. *(Please see Happiness Upgrade in this series for more information on happiness).* In that way, the behavior is inherently selfish and will likely not produce any positive results. On the other hand, however, by being 'selfish' and focusing instead on your own happiness, it is likely that you will be able to get much better results with other people. Just remember that it is not always a bad thing to focus on your own happiness over those of others.

2. Becoming downtrodden or depressed

It is not a far stretch to say that not having personal boundaries can lead to massive amounts of unhappiness and can even contribute to depression. According to Harley Therapy (2015) not having boundaries will always likely end up in frustration and depression. While the term depression is often overused in today's day and age, it is a serious concern and point of worry to avoid. A lack of happiness that can lead to a lack of desire for living life can become potentially dangerous.

In a way, personal boundaries can help to prevent depression as they are an assertion of our own self-worth. When you believe you have worth, you will likely not act in ways that will make you unhappy continuously, such as trying to keep those around you happy constantly. Depression is also often treated using chemical anti-depressants, and while we are definitely not saying that they are a bad thing and they are also very necessary in many of life circumstances, it is often better to try and avoid a chemical solution to a problem whenever possible. And so, if you have been struggling with ongoing depression it may be time to ask yourself if you lack personal boundaries. Are you letting your friends, wife or boss walk all over you or treat you in a disrespectful way and you do not want to engage them about it? If you feel depressed and the answer to the above is yes, then your problem may be a lack of boundaries.

Drawing The Line
When it comes to being assertive and creating boundaries there is a very simple, yet equally difficult thing to do, and it is using the power of the word 'no' to your advantage. This ties into what we talked about previously when it comes to doormat syndrome and being taken advantage of. Many people fall into the trap and behavioral pattern of just accepting and saying yes to any and all requests. This phenomenon is so well known that famous Hollywood actor Jim Carrey starred in a film known as 'Yes Man' (2008). In this film, Carrey loses the ability to say no to whatever anyone asks of him, and while the film is supposed to be a comedic take on the 'yes-man' conundrum, it reveals the sad truth about living such a life, that it is in the end destructive and leads to dramas being created and possibly even worse.

Of course, there are times in life where you should learn to say yes, such as new experiences and opportunities. But it is not practical nor helpful to be in the pattern of answering yes to every request you receive. But why is it not okay to say yes this often? Surely helping other people is a good thing. It is indeed if done in the right proportion. Take for example this scenario:

Your boss asks you to stay late at work because one of your colleagues is off sick and their work needs to be covered. You say yes and agree to do the extra work and an hour later receive a text from your spouse asking you to pick up dinner, which you also agree to. Now exhausted from the hours of extra work you drive the long way home in order to stop by at a supermarket. Exhausted you finally manage to get home and your children jump on you. In their excitement, they ask you to play with them and you once again say yes. With what little strength you have left you drag yourself into the living room and attempt to relax for a bit when your spouse asks you if you can make dinner.

If this little story sounds exhausting and frustrating that is because it truly is. People are just people and are only able to take on so much work at any one time. Constantly saying yes to people and not drawing the line and telling them no, will pile on responsibility and commitment at a rate which is almost impossible to keep up with. And people who are then caught in these cycles begin to self-medicate, such as with coffee or alcohol, in order to keep up with the ever-increasing workload. Saying no gives you a chance to relax and unwind. People may be annoyed at you or even try and convince you that you are a bad person for telling them no, but do not listen to them. If you do not take care of yourself then no one will and you will not be able to help effectively in the times that you do say yes. This is why you need to learn to draw the line, practice by saying no far more often than you usually do, even if it is a bit frightening at first. And remember:

"The oldest, shortest words - 'yes' and 'no' - are those which require the most thought." - Pythagoras

Developing Healthy Boundaries

When reading a book like this it can also be a trap to go far in the other direction. Putting up too many boundaries, or boundaries that are too confining it can become a strain on yourself and those around you. The real solution is to develop healthy boundaries, not too much or too little.

However, in order to do this, you will have to engage in a lot of personalized thought and good deal of personal reflection. Because everyone's boundaries and life situations are different there is unfortunately not a 'one size fits all' approach when it comes to setting up healthy boundaries, but we will aim to give you a good place to start:

1. Do you share your problems?

This is about relaxing some boundaries that you may have and that are hindering your emotional health. Many people, when they experience traumatic events such as the loss of a close friend, a family member or even being fired from their long-time job, will close up rather than express their true thoughts and feelings. They do this because they feel vulnerable and hurt and therefore do not want anyone to know about their pain. However, learning to let people in and express your feelings to them can do a world of good for your mental and even physical health. According to the National Health Service in the United Kingdom (NHS), talk therapy can help with a variety of different problems such as depression, anxiety, phobias, addiction and even some relationship problems. Therefore make sure you have healthy and looser boundaries when it comes to talking about your personal or emotional struggles. However, this should only be practiced with a licensed professional or people you deeply trust (spouse, best friend, clergy member, etc.)

2. Taking on the boss

Some people believe that because they have a superior at work they are not allowed to question them and have to accept the way they treat them no matter what. However, people who fall into this trap will often find themselves becoming more and more frustrated as time goes on and begin developing unhealthy coping mechanisms such as gossiping and slandering. It is much better to establish a healthy boundary with your boss or supervisor in order to gain their respect and also show yourself respect, as we mentioned earlier.

If your boss is treating you unfairly simply pull him aside one day when there is not much work that needs doing and ask if you can have a quick conversation with them. Explain the situation, that you think you are being treated unfairly and why you believe that and tell them that you no longer want to be treated like that. If they agree and change then the problem is solved!

However, if the problem persists then it may be worth taking it up with your HR department or even higher depending on the level of unethical behavior.

3. Get your relationships in order

Personal relationships can often be even more difficult to sort out than professional ones. This is because we care far more about these types of relationships and it is unlikely that we have a desire to hurt the people involved. However, this also means that often these are the places where personal boundaries are too loose and need to be tightened up. An example of this could be with your children, do you give them whatever they ask for because they sulk and moan or cry? If so, stop it immediately. You are not doing yourself nor them any favors in the long-term. This type of behavior will only lead to an overinflated ego and the idea that the world owes them something.

The same can be said in spousal relationships. It is not uncommon for one spouse to make the vast majority of the effort when it comes to a relationship. This is often because one partner is more afraid of losing the other. However, this type of behavior is also disrespectful and should be stopped as soon as it is recognized as a problem. If you have a spouse/partner and you are always the one planning dates, giving them compliments and doing favors for them, then reduce that behavior by an appropriate amount, start by 50% and keep reducing if nothing changes. Eventually, your partner will pick up on the change and then you can engage them in a healthy conversation about how they need to increase their activities or involvement. If they are reasonable then hopefully they will begin to see the value of the things you have been doing and therefore make a greater effort with you, the end result being that your boundary helped you be happier in two different ways.

It is also likely that standing up for yourself in this way will actually gain the respect of your partner, driving them closer rather than further away.

Rules To Live By To Keep Boundaries In Place

Having read all of this content you may be thinking to yourself "Well my problem isn't trying to set up boundaries, I just seem to not be able to keep them up for very long". Let us assure you that you are not alone in this struggle. Many people make resolutions for change, and with their good intentions, they attempt to set up boundaries only to see them fall apart a few days, weeks or months later. The problem is that the boundaries have not been put up with rules in place to assure that they stay adhered to.

It is the same as trying to lose weight. You can't just say that you are going to start dieting, and don't eat anything properly for a few days just to relapse and stuff your face with pizza for a week straight. In order to succeed you need to have a proper plan in place and heres some points that will help you achieve the result you want.

1. Write your own rules

It is human nature to think that we can make lasting change in our lives by simply telling ourselves we want to in our minds. However, this is far from the case. According to Mark Murphy of *Forbes* (2018), neuropsychologists have found that writing down your goals helps you in two ways, to more deeply internalize them to your personal memory, this phenomenon is known as 'encoding' and the fact that you have the benefit of external storage. This means that, as long as your written down goals are stored in a location where you are likely to see them often, such as on your fridge or on your computer screen, you will not need to constantly remind yourself consciously as this will do it for you.

So therefore the next time you set up, or potentially loosen, a boundary with a spouse, partner or at work, ensure that you write down exactly what the new boundary is and why you are setting it up.

2. Set up penalties

This one is pretty simple. Humans usually learn through one of two ways: rewards and pain. However, it has been shown by scientific studies that pain is actually more of a motivating force than rewards, and so if you are trying to set up permanent new boundaries you should take advantage of this phenomenon.

Whenever you have set up a new boundary, come up with a way to punish yourself if you do not stick to it. Now, we are not suggesting that you hurt yourself physically, there is no need for such drastic measures. But make sure that the punishment is uncomfortable enough to really motivate you not to break your boundary again. Some examples of this could include not allowing yourself any dessert for a few days, having to go on a 5K run or doing 200 push-ups. The punishment is really going to have to be personalized because some things may be uncomfortable for some and not at all to others. But be consistent with punishing yourself and sticking to your penalties because if you do not it is extremely unlikely you will succeed in your efforts to create healthy boundaries.

3. Always try and work together

If you are trying to set up boundaries with someone you have a personal relationship with then it is going to be helpful to get them on board. As the saying goes 'two are better than one' and two are certainly better at maintaining boundaries than just one. Whatever new measures you have agreed to with your partner and friend, make sure you hold each other to the new standard. By reminding the other person that they are not following the new boundary that they have set, it is more likely that they and you will stick to them in the future. This may cause a little bit of friction between you at times, especially if whoever you are doing this with becomes defensive when you point out their flaw, but this is something you will have to get used to if you want to be a person with strong boundaries.

Chapter Two

Everyday Assertiveness

Boundaries are not the only way for you to become assertive. Assertiveness is a comprehensive field with varying sectors, all of which you can and should take action on. However, it can be a challenge to know exactly what you are supposed to do on a daily basis to ensure that you are being assertive when you need to be. While we have already discussed some of the actions you should take in regard to boundaries, we will now discuss daily practical steps you can take to help your assertiveness in general. We will then proceed to dig just a little bit deeper.

1. Practice self-talk

This may sound strange to some people out there but hear me out. Self-talk is something that you are engaging in all the time anyway, but for many of us, it is very negative. "You are weak, you should just give up, you are useless, you can't do that, you will never be able to do that," are just some of the thoughts that people struggling with assertiveness are contending with. Positive self-talk however flips this on its head, and according to *Health Line* (2020) can have many far-reaching benefits from stress reduction to increasing confidence. And it is the last one in which we are most interested.

Next time you have a really negative thought about yourself, in relation to assertiveness, make sure you call it out. You will have to become good at monitoring your own thoughts, but with a bit of practice, it is quite easy. When you have a thought like the ones previously mentioned, tell yourself that it is a lie. Do this multiple times until you start believing that it is and to boost yourself make sure you come up with a 'counter-truth' something that you are trying to believe about yourself. So when you have a thought like 'I'm weak' you could counter with 'That's not the truth, I am strong because in the past I have...' fill in anything that backs up your claim as it will help to strengthen your belief. Practice this every day to have the most positive benefit.

2. Seek out conflict

This step is not to be misunderstood, I do not mean that you should try and start fights or arguments with people, in any way. However, being exposed to a healthy dose of conflict every day or every other day will allow you to become more assertive. Who are likely to be some of the most assertive people on the planet? The answer is soldiers and the reason they end up like that is that they go through grueling training and deal with conflict on a regular basis. A great way to do this is to engage in all the conversations you are usually afraid of having. If you are scared to tell your spouse something because they have a short-temper, say it to them. Of course, you have to manage your emotions well. You could also volunteer in high-stress environments, such as prisons or homeless shelters for the drug-addicted, in order to ensure that you get practice at being around conflict and so you learn to resolve it in a healthy manner and to grow in your assertiveness.

Being Assertive For Women

Contrary to popular belief it is not unfeminine to be assertive. A healthy amount of assertiveness is actually a key part of true mature femininity. Anyone adult should have and therefore express a certain amount of self-respect. However, women often struggle with being assertive more on average than men. For example, it has been shown in studies that women are far less likely to ask for a promotion at work.

In order to break out of your bad habits if you are a woman, or are looking to give advice to a woman you know, ensure that you understand that assertiveness does not destroy femifity. This is key because a lot of women do associate assertiveness with masculinity and therefore do not practice it. Begin to see assertiveness as a quality that is linked to maturity rather than femininity or masculinity *(as well as following all the steps in this book)* and you will see progress quickly. Just do not go too hard and being assertive because some women fall into the trap of believing they need to be assertive all the time in every scenario and that really can have a negative impact on how people come to perceive your feminity.

Being Assertive For Men

Unlike women on average, it is more likely that a man will practice being assertive. However, men face an entirely different problem than women, that problem being the mistaken belief that being aggressive is the same thing as being assertive. While it is possible to be assertive in an aggressive way, it is not advisable in any scenario. The confidence that is being displayed during a bout of assertiveness is actually undermined if it comes along with even a small dose of aggression.

Being aggressive usually indicates that you are afraid and therefore lack confidence. SO if you find that you are being aggressive a lot in your attempts to be assertive, take a deep look at the feeling of aggression in you whenever you practice, and ensure that you do not act from that place. Instead remain calm, cool and collected, confidently stating what you need to state. When you achieve this you will show true maturity, strength of character and masculinity.

Simple Steps To Be More Assertive

We have thrown a lot of information at you during the course of this book and that can become overwhelming. However, if you do not know where to start when it comes to being more assertive just follow the steps below to get started. They can give you a good foundation and from there, things can be tweaked for you as needed.

1. Say no to 1/3 of all requests made of you

As mentioned before, saying no is really important for boundaries and assertiveness so to get you used to saying no, you can start by systematically saying no to 1/3 of all requests made of you that any part of you deems unreasonable.

2. Deal with your biggest problem person

There is likely one person who you have a lot of problems being assertive with. The next time you interact with this person, make sure you stand firm on your opinions. They will push back to get you to submit, but do not let up because eventually, they will concede that you are no longer the person they once knew.

3. Do what you want a few times a week

It is likely that every day you let other people make decisions like 'where to go to lunch' or 'what movie should we watch' without giving it much thought. However, if you actually do have opinions of where to eat or what to watch and don't say anything it is just likely you are afraid of being assertive. Make sure that the very next time you find yourself in a scenario such as this that you assert your opinion and choice and insist that it is what you should go with. This may not be the best thing to do with your boss, to begin with, start with your best friend or partner.

Assertiveness and Self-Esteem

Earlier we discussed the interconnection between self-respect and boundaries. But the same is true for assertiveness in general. Being assertive means you value and care about yourself and when this is done in a healthy way and in the right amount it leads to a renewed and greater sense of self-esteem.

Many people struggle with the way they see themselves. They think they are dumb or ugly or not important. However, by becoming assertive you can start taking steps that will allow you to see yourself in a much more positive light. The journey is likely to be difficult, but it is one that will come with many benefits when carried through. A better sense of self-esteem will lead to better relationships, higher chances of financial success, as well as being able to tackle the difficult parts of life with more confidence than ever before.

There is basically no reason not to want to have a good sense of self-esteem, therefore ensure that you become more assertive and recognize how these two fields cannot be separated from one another. Do not think that fear or self-doubt have to control your life, because, with practice, they do not.

Within this first part of this book we have covered some important points to bear in mind as you make future decisions and begin to build boundaries that help you become more assertive and create a higher level and sense of self-esteem. In the secont part of this book we will dig even deep into the subject of assertiveness so you can begin to live a more assertive life with more success in it along with better relationships.

PART 2:
Your Assertive Life

Assertiveness

"If we value independence, if we are disturbed by the growing conformity of knowledge, of values, and of attitudes, which our present system induces, then we may wish to set up conditions of learning which make for uniqueness, for self-direction, and for self-initiated learning." - Carl Rogers

Assertiveness is considered an important communication skill that relates to respect for personal rights and boundaries with the intention to establish healthy and long-lasting relationships. An assertive person speaks his own mind to influence others while being respectful of the personal boundaries of others. Likewise, he protects himself against those who would cross over his own line.

Assertiveness requires direct, open, and honest communication between people. This can be between you and a work associate, a friend, or a spouse. This kind of open communication results in making everyone feel better about themselves and each other. More importantly, it will help to build, develop and maintain healthy relationships with friends, loved ones, and co-workers.

In order to develop and have healthy relationships, you need to develop communication skills, which includes being comfortable in expressing what you really need and want. This being a two-way process, you need to learn to listen to the wants and needs of others.

Up until recently, there were few books and no seminars on how to become more assertive. Most of the time, we depended on various personal or celebrity role models to lead us and show us how to live our own lives. Well, it is no wonder that everyone is still searching for happiness, pursuing fulfillment, and going after unrealistic goals.

No one has shown us how to live our lives the right way and some of our role models do not have any clue either.

Like us, no one taught them. They just relied on what they know based on how to do general things. Maya Angelou said, *"You did what you knew how to do and when you knew better, you did better."*

Fortunately for us all, not everyone is wandering around oblivious and ignorant about what to do and how best to do it. At last, there is new information available to help everyone learn more and live better. No one wants to live a cookie-cutter existence. We all want a life that is fulfilling, exciting, and most satisfying. Are you tired of waking up and thinking, "Is this all there is?"

If so, then this book is for you. Now is the absolute best time to get excited about your life! It is time to assert yourself and even start to get what you want out of life. This is your life and not a dress rehearsal! It is time to learn new skills on how to do better.

It is time to learn how to be more assertive.

Chapter Three

What's Stopping You From Becoming Assertive?

"Assertiveness is not about what you do, it's about who you are!"
- Shakti Gawain

There is a huge difference between being assertive and being aggressive. Being assertive is a way of living where you get the most out of life without other people telling you how to do it. This simply means: You do not need to be obnoxious, pushy, or rude to get things your own way. In fact, quite the opposite is true.

You cannot just jump in with both feet and decide, *"Hey, I'm going to be assertive and no one will be pushing me around anymore. No more Mr. Nice Guy!"* Learning how to be assertive requires a new mindset and a specific plan. Remember, you want to learn to be assertive, not become more aggressive. So, ask yourself these questions:

1. What do I value most?

2. What are my beliefs about how life works?

3. How do I feel about myself?

4. What are my approaches to life? Do these approaches work?

The fact that you purchased this program says a lot. It says you are looking for some improvements in your life. Change starts with awareness. You are aware that you need to change; you just do not know how to get started. It is time to learn why you do what you are doing and how to turn that around to get more of what you want.

Remember, you cannot just flip a switch and instantly become assertive and successful in life.

Mark Twain said, *"We do not deal very much in facts when we are contemplating ourselves."* In order to learn how you can become more assertive and be in charge of your own life, you must be honest with yourself. Dr. Phil is always saying that you cannot change what you do not acknowledge. It is time to figure out what you are hiding from yourself. The following questions may start to shed a little light on the subject of you.

- Do you consistently fail when it comes to attaining your goals in life?

- Are you just drifting along with no plan, goals, and ideas?

- Are you stuck in a comfort zone that gives you no new challenges?

- Are you getting too little of what you really want and way too much of what you do not want?

- Are you living with guilt or frustration and do not know how to change things?

If you have found answers to those questions then begin to ask yourself why? What is at stake here is the quality of your life. Do you want to live it fully and authentically? Or are you okay with someone else calling the shots and making decisions for you for the rest of your life?

Do you feel like you are constantly being pushed around? Do you feel like you are being taken advantage of? Do other people try to run your life? Do you feel that you are ready to start living life on your own terms?

You need not accept burdens like those listed above. You can assert yourself and reach for something better. You have the right and the ability to get what you want out of life. Let me warn you though, change does not come in an instant.

Assertiveness is something that must be learned carefully one single step at a time. This is especially true if you have spent years following others telling you what to do, and how to do it, what to think, and what to feel, etc.

How motivated are you to change and learn to assert yourself?

Think about those people who run our world. Whether it is in business, politics, sports, or entertainment, there is one common denominator for all these people. These people know which buttons to push to get what they want. Some of these people are extremely intelligent and articulate, while others are merely manipulative. Some are unconcerned whether you agree with them and share their views. Others are rabid in demanding that you fall in line with them. They feel that they know best and this gives them the authority to tell everyone what they should be doing and saying. It is their way or the highway.

Be aware that there are risks involved in learning how to be assertive. You will find that many will not agree with you. In fact, you will meet people who are skeptical and pessimistic. They will always argue and try to prove you wrong.

Let us continue with your assessment in life by acknowledging what is wrong in your own personal life. Are you guilty of stating or repeating these things to yourself?

- I'm really trying but you know, it's just so hard!
- I guess it could have been much worse.
- It's not what I wanted, but what am I going to do?
- Sometimes you just have to do what you have to do.
- We're doing okay, I guess.

Are you making lots of excuses? such as:

- It was harder than I expected, I just couldn't do it.
- Maybe I was expecting too much.
- I have too much going on in my life to handle any of this right now.
- I'll tackle that as soon as I have the time and resources.
- I guess what I wanted isn't meant for me.
- Maybe it's not in the cards. It's not my destiny.
- I never seem to get the right break.

It is time to stop whining about bad luck, wrong timing, or how things just never seem to work out for you! Stop hosting self-pity parties! Realize that the deck is not stacked against you! Stop making excuses! It is time to learn to assert yourself and get what you really, really want!

So, remember this, in its most simple form: *"Luck and Success are when Preparedness Meets Opportunity."*

So... PREPARE First.

Okay, let us get down to basics. What exactly are you afraid of? That is easy. People share a universal fear of rejection. The very thought of being rejected can turn the strongest man or woman into a quivering coward.

What does everyone crave for in life? This one is also easy. We all crave for acceptance. We feel lost if we are not accepted. We feel left out, excluded, and ostracized. Acceptance is everything.

We learn about acceptance from infancy. Children will go to any lengths; even do things they dislike just to gain the acceptance of their parents, friends, or teachers. These patterns will continue throughout our lives as we grow.

Paul Landres gives us an example of the mindset of an assertive person when he said, *"And is the price for your acceptance for me to conform? To be as you would want me to be? You must accept me as I am."*

So, accepted or not and rejected or not, you have your own destiny to create. You can make it happy or sad, good or bad, successful or not. Your life is your own and ultimately, you are responsible for how it turns out.

There may be road bumps along the way and not everything will turn out according to your plan. You may have to adjust your road map and come up with a Plan B or even a Plan C along the way. In the end, learning how to be assertive will help you to win more often and help you to get what you want.

Without assertiveness, you will lose control of your life and find yourself living someone else's idea of what life should be. If you shy away from being accountable and taking charge of your own life, someone will step forward to claim responsibility for it.

This could be a parent, spouse, or in the case of an elderly person, maybe one of their own children.
If you never master the ability to assert yourself, make your own decisions, and live your own life, someone will surely step forward and do it for you. Is that what you want?

Asserting yourself also does not mean blaming others for your decisions. *For example: "My husband left me with nothing when he died, so it's not my fault that I'll have to live with my children for the rest of my life."*

Rather than take the responsibility for your own decisions, you choose to volunteer for victim-hood and blame someone else.

Asserting yourself and taking full responsibility is scary and risky for anyone. "What if I assert myself and try to create my own destiny and it doesn't work out? Then, what will I do?" It is normal to be a little fearful because it is part of human nature. Keep in mind that all decisions have consequences. As you learn to be more assertive, you also learn to trust yourself when making decisions.

Your thoughts influence your world. *"There is nothing either good or bad, but thinking makes it so,"* said William Shakespeare. To think is to create.

Your thoughts create your reality. Your thoughts influence your actions and behavior. A change in your thoughts leads to a change in behavior and eventually in your world. What do you consistently tell yourself? Do these negative statements sound familiar?

- I'm just not smart enough.
- I've never succeeded before, why would now be any different?
- People refuse to listen to people like me.
- People make up their minds and there's nothing I can do about it.
- I'm too young or too old.

Start by choosing to learn how to be more assertive starting today. With this, you will need a well thought out plan. There will be days when you wonder if you can sustain and follow through your plan. Wouldn't it be easier to just throw in the towel and be done with it?

If you find yourself in this position, remind yourself of the benefits you will enjoy when you become assertive. Keeping the benefits in mind will help in sustaining your new and assertive behavior.

Others may be in a difficult situation. This is especially true of the elderly. It is hard for them to persevere, especially when the children try to control their lives and make decisions for them.

There are many variables here. Each person must evaluate and decide what is important and what isn't. Being assertive means choosing for yourself where you want to be and with whom. It means choosing what to do, what to say, and what to believe.

What is keeping you from being more assertive? What keeps you from making your own decisions? Are you afraid you won't be any good at it? Are you secretly afraid that you will be so good at it that your entire life will change? St. Paul said, *"I do not understand my own actions. For I do not do what I want, but I do the very thing I hate."*

Assertiveness is a learned behavior. Probably, it was not taught to you as you were growing up. Unknowingly, you developed certain behavioral patterns that do not support assertiveness. You fall into a trap where you constantly wonder why your life is not what you wanted.

The definition of insanity is doing the same things in the same way, but expecting different outcomes. If you have never done so before, learning to assert yourself produces a change in how you handle yourself.

Assert yourself by doing things in different ways and produce a different outcome. Presto, you have just asserted yourself and changed your life! Learn this important lesson from Dr. Phil McGraw when he said, *"If you continue to do what you've always done, you will continue to have what you've always had. If you do different, you will have different."*

Unfortunately, some of the behavioral patterns that you learned in life become automatic. You do not even have to think about your response anymore. You do not allow yourself to evaluate the cause and effect of this behavior; you are just flying on autopilot. It may seem easier to completely let go and not to think about the consequences. In the end, you will realize that certain behavior patterns will not continue to work for you.

By remaining static and not changing the pattern of behavior, you repeat the old patterns repeatedly. It is important to stop, think, and re-evaluate whether a learned behavior is really working for you or has become another crutch to keep you in homeostasis. This is covered deeply in freedom from addictions which also includes steps to remove anything that isn't working for you and serving your best interests.

There is a reason why you keep getting stuck and unable to move forward. When you continue to repeat a bad pattern repeatedly, you are doing it for a reason. You must find the reason in order to change the behavior. Change the behavior in order to change your life for the better.

Some people seem to be at the mercy of others, unable to make their own decisions or are not in charge of their own lives. They let others push them around by telling them what to do and how to do it. The sad part is that they have allowed this to happen for several years in most cases. Some of these folks may never find their own way, while others may just snap one day and tell everyone off in a not so subtle manner.

This kind of abrupt behavioral change leaves everyone concerned, puzzled, and will lead to destroyed relationships and damaged friendships.

When you decide to be assertive, you must also realize that this learned behavior must be reinforced every day. Assertiveness is not a cure-all for all your ill feelings. It is a way of managing your life.

The University of Illinois Counseling Center says that, *"Asserting yourself will not necessarily guarantee you happiness or fair treatment by others, nor will it solve all your personal problems or guarantee that others will be assertive and not aggressive. Just because you assert yourself does not mean you will always get what you want; however, lack of assertiveness is most certainly one of the reasons why conflicts occur in relationships."*

Reciprocity should work alongside assertiveness, too. Choosing to make your own decisions does not require you to damage another person. Being assertive does not give you permission to push another aside, take over another's life, or make decisions for them.

Assertiveness is about you and your own life. It is all about your decisions and the consequences of those decisions. Let us correct a misconception here. Assertiveness is all about getting what you want AND building a lasting relationship with people around you.

Assertiveness works fine when used with diplomacy. You can assert yourself without hurting others' feelings. In fact, the real essence of assertiveness is this: As you get what you want in life, you gain the support of people who would like and even love to see you succeed.

Chapter Four

Assertiveness in the Work Place:

Don't Confuse Assertiveness with Aggressiveness!

"The basic difference between being assertive and aggressive is how our words and behavior affect the rights and well-being of others." - Sharon Anthony Bower

Oprah Winfrey calls it *"the disease to please"*. Nowhere, except for a woman's world, does it run more rampant than in the workplace. There is a special pressure in the workplace from your boss, supervisor, your associates, and co-workers. Everyone is usually extremely busy these days. This disease seems to attack women more frequently, but men can be affected by it too.

Assertiveness should not be confused with aggressiveness. A fine line divides these two behaviors. Being aggressive means selfishly pushing for what you want at the expense of other people. In doing so, you generate a host of negative behaviors that make people become angry and vengeful towards you. It may involve hostility, blaming, threats, gossip, and unreasonable demands. Aggressiveness may allow you to achieve your most immediate objective, but it also guarantees that you will not have what you want the next time around or at a later date.

On the other hand, assertiveness means standing up for your rights while respecting the rights of others. Being assertive means the appropriate expression of your own feelings, needs, and opinions while still respecting the feelings of others around you. It is communicating what you really want in a clear way while ensuring that you are not being taken advantage of by someone trying to serve their own needs at the expense of your own.

Let us say your boss asks you to do a special favor for him. Now here is the potential problem: that little favor is beyond your job description. In fact, it is within the scope of his duty as the Boss. Now you have a dilemma. Do you say "no" because it is not your responsibility to do his job, thereby run the risk of incurring his anger? Or do you say yes just to avoid making him angry? After all, you need this job desperately considering the mountains of bills that you have to pay monthly; thus, you really can't afford to make him angry.

On the other hand, you know very well that if you do his job the first time, it is most likely that he will be asking you to do things that he should be doing himself. This will eventually develop into a pattern. You do it this time and he will just keep on turning over his responsibilities to you. Before you know it, a habit is formed and you become stuck.

If previously you gave in to some of his requests, saying "no" now would most likely make him mad at you. After all, you have been doing it before, why not do it again this time?

So, what is the answer? Be assertive right at the beginning and in all instances until the Boss realizes that you cannot be pushed around. You do not need to get nasty or abusive with him. In fact, you will probably lose your job if you do!

Be assertive right at the beginning when he asks you to take over some project that he should be doing. You could tell him, *"I'd love to help you out, but I'm just swamped with my own work already. I couldn't possibly do justice to your project that it so rightfully deserves."*

Go ahead and check the language used above and you will find out that you have not directly said no to him or embarrassed him so he cannot be too angry with you.

You have acknowledged that his project is worthy of attention, but gently nudged him into remembering that it is his project and that it is his duty to finish it, not yours.

What you have done here is set a precedence that he will remember. You did not blindly just say yes to avoid his anger. He is the Boss and would have taken advantage of your skills many times in the future. For example, every time he has a project that he did not want to tackle himself, he will just pass it on to you. Now he knows he cannot just dump his duties on your lap all the time. You may have to repeat this action a couple more times before he gets the message.

The same scenario should work with co-workers who try to pass on the jobs they do not want to do. This trick is used mercilessly on newcomers in the office. Newcomers try so hard to please everyone that they get stuck with all the less desirable tasks and find themselves with very little time to accomplish the duties they were actually hired to perform.

Why do people continue to say "yes" when they want to say "no"? There are many reasons actually. One reason is that they want people to like them. They are afraid that if they say "no", they will have no friends at all. They are also afraid that the boss will use their refusal as a ground for insubordination, and thereby dismiss them.

One reason why people are continually doing this is that they want to be known as the "go-to" person. They want to develop a good reputation and be known as dependable and can always accomplish the task. It makes them feel wanted, needed, and much more valuable to the organization. If you want something accomplished, just take it to these "go-to" persons and consider it already done! It makes them feel good when they feel like you cannot do without them. After all, if everyone needs them, then their job must be secure, right?

Unfortunately, this inability to say "no" can work to your own detriment. It causes a build-up of stress hormones, such as adrenaline. As a result, your heart will beat faster than its normal pace, your blood pressure rises, and blood vessels become narrow.

According to doctors, these conditions can increase your risk of heart attack, stroke, and even cancer. Saying "yes" to others all the time could put you in an early grave!

In the early days of man, these stress hormones could literally save lives. During the pre-historic times, people lived in a 'fight or flight' world. It is either they hunt or be hunted. Adrenaline saved them from danger.

Nowadays, danger is present in the way that you eat and in the lifestyle that you live. Many become couch potatoes and worry constantly. The stress you experience these days is different but just as deadly.

Therefore, the answer is to stop being a doormat and learn to say *"no"* more often. I can almost hear your gasps and objections to that statement. I anticipate your reactions: *"Wait a minute, you do not know the situation I am in"* or *"You just do not know how to be unemployed".*

You might be afraid to say *"no",* but sometimes it is necessary. For starters, those people who already like you are not going to stop liking you just because you said *"no".* Those who behave in a grumpy manner were like that long before you told them so.

Okay, so you mustered all your courage and said *"no",* but now you feel guilty for doing so. How do you handle that? You probably feel like you let them down. Guilt is not necessary here; it is a useless emotion and one of the most destructive which is why it has been used for thousands of years as a weapon.

Stop and think about how you really feel when they ask you to do them a favor. Did you say *"yes"* then feel resentful about it? If that is the case, now you have a cue that when this situation happens again, say *"no"* right away. Do not makeup excuses that you both know are lies. It will make you feel guilty for saying something deceitful and wrong. You could tell them that:

You're right in the middle of some projects and simply don't have the time.

You'd rather tell them *"no"* than only be able to give it a fraction of your attention.

You're really not the best person for that job.

Your calendar is full right now and so you can't take on any more tasks.

If they surprised you with the request and you do not know what to say, ask them to give you some time to think about it and consult your calendar. Many times, they will ask you without any warning, hoping you will just say *"yes"* right away.

Learn to always give yourself a little wiggle room or flexibility. When you do decide to inform them of your negative decision, say it right off the bat, so they understand they cannot talk you into a *"yes"*. Being definite about your response at the soonest possible time will make them respect you more and may cause fewer hurt feelings later.

Somehow, we have been led to believe that it is hurtful to say *"no"*. You have been taught that you have to be nice to everyone and say *"yes"* even when you don't want to. This is especially true for women.

Think of it this way: Is the other person's time more valuable than your own?

Is it necessary to bend over backward to avoid saying *"no"* and just take in everything at your expense?

Think of the possible consequences.
Eventually, you will find yourself gradually building more resentment towards the person making the request. Everything he asks you to do then becomes another nail in the coffin!

It is actually better for you to say *"no"* to everyone involved and save a working relationship, not to mention your own nerves and stress level. Keep in mind that the more often you say *"yes"* the more often they will ask you for more favors. Therefore, you should only say *"yes"* if it is something that you truly would like to do for them. You can say *"yes"* if it is something that you can conveniently fit into your schedule without causing any wear and tear on your nerves.

People are basically good and you would like to help people whenever you can, but so many *"yeses"* can turn into more than you can handle. You have heard the phrase, *"No good deed goes unpunished."*

Recognize that there are limits to everyone's time and energy. The *disease to please* somehow convinces you that you can fit more in each day than anyone else. You will discover this reality when you realize you do not have time to do more than a shoddy job. You will discover this truth when you begin to feel overwhelmed and realize that your commitments are way past your own personal limits. It is simply better for all involved if you just say *"no"* at the beginning. By telling them right away, they have a chance to find someone else who can help them.

Remember, they have the right to ask a favor, but you also have the right to say *"no"*. Do not give up your rights just because you want them to like you. They will respect you more if they see you know how to handle things properly and without overtaxing yourself or stressing others out.

You may have decided that asserting yourself is a good idea, but do not know how to apply it in scenarios involving confrontations. Confrontation involves getting in the other person's face and not taking into consideration their feelings. You probably would not want to hurt the other persons' feelings, right?

So, what do you do? Many people avoid confrontation altogether, which is not always a good idea. Sometimes, it is much easier to approach the person as gently as possible, say what you have to say and get it over with.

Approaching the issue with more assertion and without anger is always best. This is true even if you feel you are the aggrieved party and need to defend yourself. Many people use this as a last resort when all else had previously failed. It is important to simply lay out the problem, enumerate what you think needs to be resolved and find a compromise by which everyone gets what they need.

One way to bring this about is not to approach confrontation in a heated manner. This needs to be well thought out in advance. Have a plan. You should have everything you feel and want to say planned out in your mind or written down on paper as a reference during the discussion. Be fully prepared and ready to face the consequences when this confrontation is over. It could be the end of your job or a friendship.

Again, you have the right to assert yourself. This is your life and your workplace. It should not be a place where you dread going to each day. Everyone needs to have personal standards for how they treat themselves and how others treat them. Boundaries have to be set and maintained even in the workplace. We will discuss more on boundaries later on.

Assertiveness, not aggressiveness, is what is essential for you to feel better about yourself and also develop better relations with others.
It will also help keep the unpleasant or discomfort levels to a minimum, relieve stress, and maybe even move your career forward. Learning to be assertive could even move you into a leadership position one day.

Remember, while assertiveness can help you get what you want out of life, aggression will bring about resignation or involuntary compliance on the part of those around you. We are talking about the best-case scenario. The worst case is that they resent you, resist anything you want from them, and maybe show downright hostility to boot. This is not what you want at all. Aggression simply decreases your chances of getting what you really want.

Aggression will only bring in fear, threats, and hostility because of manipulation, where you force and coerce people to do it your way. You cannot always make someone give in to what you want. As they say, "You might win the battle, but you will lose the war."

Pushing someone into doing something they do not wish to do may result in grudging compliance at first, but you will not win them over in the end. They may give in just to get you to shut up and go away. You have not won them to your side if that is the case. With the passive-aggressive types, you might even find yourself on the receiving end of an object lesson.

True assertiveness means without aggression, guilt, and fear. It is far more effective in the long run and infinitely more satisfying. Winning others to your way of thinking, the legitimate way is much more fun!

Chapter Five

Assertiveness at Home:

Teach People How to Treat You!

"When I'm trusting and being more myself as fully as possible, everything in my own personal life reflects this by falling into place easily, often miraculously." - Shakti Gawain

Assertiveness has its place at home, as well as, in any other place. Wherever humans gather, there will always be a need for well-placed assertiveness. Just as there is a need for boundaries in the workplace, so there is also a need for boundaries at home.

A boundary is a line that you draw between yourself and others; this includes even loved ones. It is a line that represents physical and emotional limits. You draw the line to indicate that going beyond that means a violation of your standards and rights. It may sound strange to think of boundaries between family members, but it is essential for a healthy and happy family.

All members need to know their limits when dealing with you and that same boundary protects them too. Setting boundaries can make you feel safe and make others feel safe, too. Everyone should know what to expect and have relevant information about the wants and needs of everyone.

Stop and think about the times you felt uncomfortable, hurt, angry, or even betrayed. Those dark emotions indicate that your boundaries were somehow crossed. This clearly shows the need for everyone to have those boundaries.

Boundaries ensure that your rights are protected. You have the right to enjoy positive and satisfying relationships. This type of relationship allows you to express yourself honestly and also informs others how you wish to be treated.

I think you would be surprised to know that many couples simply do not know how to treat each other because they do not know what they want. If you want your spouse to treat you with a little consideration and respect, you have to tell him/her. It seems so obvious and simple. Your spouse would not know if you do not tell them. You must teach them how to treat you.

There are times when being assertive towards your spouse may seem like an uphill battle. It just feels like he/she is not listening to what you are saying; it seems like he/she is not attentive to your needs. Approaching them in the same old manner may be your problem. It is time to find a new way to say what you need to say.

Many men and women approach their spouse with the old guilt trip starting with negative feelings, feelings of superiority, and blame. Remember how your grandmother used to tell you how you could catch more flies with honey than with vinegar? The same thing applies here. If you start with the blame game, your spouse is going to shut down within thirty seconds. He/she has heard all this before and will tune out as soon as you open your mouth. It is time to try a new tactic.

Put aside those negative feelings and do not start with a criticism. Try to see things from your spouse's point of view and find again the good things that you once loved about that particular person. Appreciate his/her good points and put aside the issues you two fight about.

Approach the encounter very carefully, always keep calm, and most importantly, watch your language.

Always remember that ill-chosen words can hurt deeply. Avoid blaming the other person. Try to be supportive of your spouse and for heaven's sake, admit when you are wrong!

Asserting yourself and negotiating does not mean tearing the other person down all for the purpose of proving that you are right and the other party is wrong. Making your spouse feel miserable and unworthy is no way to negotiate your wants and needs. That is not a win-win situation. Instead, try to look at your spouse's positive points and boost his/her general morale. Abraham Lincoln said, *"It is difficult to make a man miserable while he feels he's worthy of himself."*

Sometimes, the problem is not your spouse but another member of your family or your spouse's family. Keep in mind that you are living your own life now with your partner and children as a family. Do not let relatives or in-laws push you around. You will encounter some family members that practically insist on a fight. It is better to politely avoid an argument and simply refuse to be pulled into any form of discussion or confrontation. Keep it simple and try these deflections:

- I'm going to bow out of this one, thanks.

- Sorry, I don't have an opinion on that.

- I truly wish I had something to contribute to this, but I don't.

- Maybe you could rephrase that, please.

- Leave me out of this.

Goethe told us that, *"Behavior is a mirror in which everyone shows his image."*

It is good to keep in mind that we are all created equal and should treat each other accordingly. Do not be recklessly assertive and go overboard when dealing with a loved one. When dealing with those you are closest to, learn to how be more assertive and less aggressive. Be more confident and less fearful.

Learn to be more effective so you will not come off as wishy-washy. Stop being a fence sitter; say what you feel and mean what you say. Demanding to have everything your way will not earn you the respect you desire from your family. Being calmly assertive and fair with everyone will command that respect. It will even encourage them to emulate you.

Boundaries must be set and adhered to at all times in order for families to be happy, healthy, and respectful of each other family member. Asserting your rights within the family is not asking too much and makes for a better relationship. Boundaries would include making sure each member of the family has needed privacy and space. It also has to do with how each member speaks to the others in the family. Negative, insulting, or rude talk is not acceptable.

It is unfortunate that some people allow others to decide for them and then become bitter in the end. This is especially true within the framework of a family. One spouse begins making the decisions for the entire family, without necessarily consulting the other. If you find this to be true in your own household, keep in mind that your partner began making those decisions because you allowed that to happen in the first place.

Many spouses let their partners have it their own way to maintain the peace in the family. This can absolutely work to your personal disadvantage. The longer that you allow it to continue, the more difficult it becomes to assert yourself, take back your own life, and exercise your decision-making capabilities.

This whole dynamic can lead to low self-esteem and feelings of inferiority since you allow others to decide matters for you. Their actions are inferring that you are not capable of making your own decisions.

Eleanor Roosevelt once said, *"No one can make you feel inferior without your own consent."* If your spouse has begun taking the initiative and is making decisions that you do not agree with, guess whose fault it is?

By your inaction, you have taught your partner that it is okay to go over your head and decide what you should have and not have. You have given away your power but you can still get it back. You will find in the last chapter of this book a short assertiveness training section to help you regain your power of decision making.

If people in your life are treating you badly, you must figure out things that you are doing which allow them to continue behaving in such ways. What is it that makes them feel free to verbally or physically abuse you?

Women may find themselves feeling uncomfortable around men who curse, have potty mouths, or tend to talk about women in unacceptable terms. Men who behave this way have no respect for women. By remaining silent, these women are allowing this behavior to perpetuate.

Sometimes men act this way with the intention of putting the woman in her place and make her feel subjugated. Some guys truly do not have a clue that they are creating an uncomfortable atmosphere for women to live with.

Women will have to be assertive and teach these men to treat women with respect. They must insist on putting an end to this kind of talk. Sometimes, a simple reminder such as: *"Excuse me, Lady in the room,"* is enough to get their attention.

One of the biggest roadblocks to asserting yourself could be an unarticulated desire. Many people may want something from someone but are unclear, even in their own minds, on exactly what that "something" is. They make no verbal assertions about their wants and needs, but rather expect others to instinctively know what that mysterious "something" could be.

While we are all about improving ourselves by learning new skills and developing new talents, most of us are simply not capable of reading the minds of others (outside of the amazing Kreskin, that is!). People cannot possibly grant that mysterious "something" to you if they do not have a clue what it is.

Stop waiting for your spouse, kids, boss, co-workers, or friends to magically figure out what you want or need. Assert yourself and tell them clearly what you need. Remember that assertiveness is about getting what you need and protecting your rights, while not stomping on the feelings and rights of others. So, open your mouth and say what you need. If you want to reap the benefits, you must first give it a name. You must articulate whatever it is that you want, need, or desire.

Maybe the simple act of making a decision is what is holding you back. Indecision keeps you from articulating what you truly want and need. Indecision causes homeostasis, inaction, and resistance to change. If you do not decide, someone will eventually decide for you and you probably would not like the result.

Knowing what you really want is essential. In this world, the only thing you will get is exactly what you ask for. What are you asking for?

Chapter Six

Teach Your Children to Be Assertive:

Create Confident Offspring

"When children are treated with acceptance, they develop self-acceptance." - Stephanie Matson

Children often experience pressure at home. For sure, they also experience pressure in school. So, it is not too early to teach them to be assertive. Keep in mind that teaching them to be assertive is not the same thing as teaching them to be more aggressive or obnoxious. It does not mean teaching them to go on the offensive.

This started for us when we were children and continued into our adult life. The situation is more difficult for children as they are not yet aware that they have individual rights, the same as we adults do. Children (and even adults!) need to be taught that:

No one has the right to make them feel guilty, feel foolish, or to feel ignorant.

Though some may try to do just that, your child needs to know that those bullies do not have the right to do such mean things to anyone. They should be avoided and ignored and not listened to for the sake of your child's well-being.

Children do not need to make excuses to everyone for every little thing they may do and every choice they make.

Children are accountable only to few people and these are mainly their parents, brothers, sisters, close relatives and the immediate family. Of course, they are also accountable to themselves but no one else.

They are allowed to change their minds at any time and to not feel bad about it.

Sometimes, adults have a change of heart. So why can't kids have the same? They need to know that it is quite okay to change their minds. Nothing is carved in stone, especially when it comes to children.

If things go wrong, it is not necessarily their fault.

Many children internalize family problems. They take the blame for things they have no control of. In fact, these are often things that they should not deal with at all. An example of this is the separation of their parents.

They do not have to know everything. It is okay for them to say, *"I do not know"* or *"I do not understand"*.

Adults do not know everything so why should a small child be any different? It is important to teach your child not to feel inferior because they do not have the right answers to all of the questions they may face in life available to them. Children often feel this way in the early years of school. They need to be reminded that their lack of knowledge is the primary reason why they have to study in school! In this, school is really a means to an end. Of facilitating the thinking processes to better enable them to more easily cope with personal and life situations.

Making a mistake is not the end of the world.

There is nothing wrong about committing mistakes. Children need to know that no one is perfect and we all make mistakes. They should just admit the mistake and correct it, if possible. Mistakes are mechanisms that facilitate learning.

They do not have to be everybody's friend.

Not everyone is going to like every child, but that is okay. Many children feel that there is something wrong with them if they have few friends in school. This is one of the basic lessons for children. Somewhere along the way, they are going to meet other kids who will not like them. It is the same in the adult world, isn't it?

If they do not understand something, it is okay to say, "I don't get it."

Children feel bad if they do not get it or they do not understand something. They can actually think that they are inferior and that there is something very wrong with them. Not everybody can understand everything all at once in the early years of life. Life experience always leads to better understanding through the process of living and including the mistakes we make along the way, but it is perfectly okay so long as the journey is one of gaining more knowledge and understanding of the things around us which eventually leads to greater wisdom.

They do not have to prove themselves to everyone they meet.

Children need to be taught and to understand that they do not have to prove anything to others. It is okay just to be themselves. Having to prove something to everyone is exhausting and will sap the self-confidence you are trying to build in your child.

They do not have to be perfect.

Perfection is not possible anyway. They should just be themselves. It is unfair to expect perfection from your child when you cannot attain it yourself.

The biggest obstacle to your children's personality development might just be their own social skills. Young children have social and communication skills that they can build over time to make them feel more self-confident.

Although sometimes meeting new kids makes many children a little nervous, it can also lead to more confidence, a wider circle of friends and a much wider perspective. The process can even make some child unsure about themselves, what to say or how to say it, how to approach other children and even adults if they do not go through the process from time to time.

You can prepare them for possible new social encounters by doing frequent little role-playing activities with them. Help them begin to practice social conversation by pretending to be the new kid. Teach your child how to initiate and sustain a conversation with others.

Teaching them social skills is the first step to making them more comfortable in just about any given life situation. The more comfortable they feel in these situations, the easier they will learn how to be assertive. The better they understand themselves, the more they will know and articulate their needs.

As you go about the role-playing activities, you must teach your children how to ask questions and get others to respond. Also, equip them with skills on following up on the information that they receive. This will teach your kids to become good listeners. This is especially helpful for shy children. This way, you develop children to become good listeners, excellent conversationalists, self-confident and assertive individuals.

Because of their young age, frustration can easily get set in and then there can very easily be a tendency to respond with anger. It is imperative to teach your children that anger is not a good tool for asserting themselves. As an adult, you already know that other people react negatively towards anger and aggressiveness. Anger distorts the message the child is trying to deliver, thus resulting in a break-down in communication. Just as this is highly ineffective for adults, so it is also with children. Credibility is automatically discounted when they display anger with others.

Children are more expressive in communicating anger. Signs of anger may include dragging their feet (being passive-aggressive), throwing tantrums, breaking toys, or even hitting others. It may be hard to understand, especially for young children, that anger is not an effective tool in building assertiveness.

When you are asserting your authority over children, one of the qualities that you should have is persistence. Repetition is another effective way of teaching young toddlers. You repeat over and over what you want them to learn. Your children can use the same tool to help assert themselves to their peers. Yelling, screaming, and pounding will not get them what they want, but persistence will wear down the opposition. It will also help your child make and keep friends as they generally become a good influence on others around them.

Another useful tool is working out a compromise with others. Everyone wants to feel they won the last round.

A compromise ensures that both sides win and nobody loses. Asserting without denying the rights of the other person can bring about a peaceful solution for everyone.

In the art of negotiation, the purpose is not to win and watch another person lose, simply because true negotiating is not a competition. Successful negotiating should always be a win-win situation or outcome to consistently pursue in every negotiation and life situation. If only for the simple reason that if you bully your way to the top no one will be willing to support you or your child when they get there, often resulting in fall at some point.

Non-assertive children will become oversensitive to criticisms, especially those expressed by family members. They are also terrified of getting caught making a mistake. They are constantly afraid of being wrong, doing something wrong, or being thought of as stupid because the school system can have that effect.
You can also spot non-assertive children because of their lack of persistence. They give up far too easily and do not try after a single failure.

Children must be taught to deal with mistakes. They have to know that it is not the end of the world if they make an error. Everybody makes mistakes, so it is okay as long as you admit and try to rectify it. When children are not taught how to cope with mistakes, they tend to get extremely upset as they begin fighting themselves. And in effect NOT being their own best friend which should always be the case as not being your best friend results in negative self-talk which leads to negative experiences.

Learning to deal with one's own faults and those of others is difficult enough for adults to deal with, let alone children. Let them know it is okay not to be perfect, none of us are. You should not expect them to perform perfectly all the time. Perfection is something none of us can live up to, no matter how hard we try.

It is unfair to expect a child to be perfect. Many children spend their whole lives trying to live up to their parents' often unfair expectations, instead of learning to be the best at whatever they choose.

That isn't to say that the goal should be to strive for perfection which results in producing the very best results we can achieve in any particular area.

As far as criticism is concerned, you should prepare your children in handling them. They will receive criticisms all throughout their lives. There will always be somebody around to criticize them. The critics are out there waiting to pounce on them for any slight imperfection or error. When children learn to relax, and just be themselves, filter what others have to say, and learn not to be easily influenced by opinions of others, they will lead a happier and more relaxed life. They will then more easily grow up and become well-adjusted adults in the future.

Keep in mind that the only way you will be able to teach your children how to assert themselves is by learning how to be assertive yourself and passing on the experience of what that is.

As much as you want your children to be assertive and learn to stand up for themselves, you should not become a pushover parent in the process. As suggested, aggressiveness or general rudeness is not a good classification of being assertive.

If you find it hard to say "no" to your children when they are making unreasonable demands, and if you give in repeatedly, you are setting the stage for their demands to grow larger and larger with each passing day. It is up to you as the adult to set the good example for your child. No means no, period, end of discussion. You do not need to become a doormat to ensure that your child becomes assertive.

Be a good role model for your children. Children learn what they see and experience. If you are assertive and fair, they will learn to become assertive and fair, too. Always keep in mind what John W. Whitehead said, *"Children are the living messages we send to a time we will not see."*

Chapter Seven

Assertiveness Training for the Non-Assertive

"What lies behind us and what lies before us are tiny matters compared to what lies within us." - Ralph Waldo Emerson

Shakti Gawain taught us, *"You create your opportunities by asking for them."* In this section of the book, I'm going to show you how you can become more assertive and more in control of your life.

We will concentrate on assertiveness training that will help you in your career and other types of social encounters. Non-assertive people encounter many difficulties when it comes to their business or careers. People grapple with the right words in the right situation and would not have any idea on how to fast track their climb in the corporate or business ladder.

The first part of the assertiveness training is geared towards showing you how to get control of yourself, how to be less shy, and become more expressive towards others.

The second part of the training will show you how to influence others and how to have a better understanding of other's behavior towards you, particularly those that mistreat you or take advantage of you.

According to the Merriam-Webster Dictionary, *"Assertiveness enables individuals to act in a bold and self-confident manner."* Whether it is on the job or at home, you are dealing with people. These people include customers, co-workers, supervisors, the boss, doctors, dentists, nurses, repairmen, installers, teachers, principals, banker, etc. that you encounter on a regular basis. Lack of assertiveness can cause a number of problems, as you may have personally discovered.

Maybe you are tired of always saying *"yes"* to everyone and then feeling resentful later. Maybe you are tired of everyone taking advantage of your good nature. Maybe you are just plain tired because nobody is listening to your opinions and thoughts, as if you are not even there.

If you identified with any one or more of the above situations, there is a solution. The steps are easy to follow, but you will need to practice every day. Repetitions are necessary for you and for those you deal with on a regular basis.

Once you have mastered the basics of assertiveness, you will begin to notice a difference right away. People will listen to you more closely, once you have grabbed their attention assertively.

You will start to gain the respect you know you deserve. Best of all, you will feel better about yourself. You will feel less shy and more confident about yourself and your abilities.

You will no longer fear confrontations and learn to say *"no"* with ease and without guilt. You will learn to stay calm, even when people are arguing with you. You will realize that you need not be rushed into making decisions. You will avoid agreeing with things that you do not really want to. With more confidence in your own assertiveness, your stress level will drop dramatically.

First of all, we will work on your self-confidence. Self-confidence is built by undergoing a series of experiences that affirm your self-worth. Every time you try to do something new, you will gain new experience and perspectives in life. It does not matter if what you experienced resulted in failure, you will still come out as a winner as long as you learn something from it.

Always keep in mind that a failure or mistake is temporary. For the experience to become useful, you must learn from it.

Everything that you will learn from this assertiveness training should be practiced every day, possibly with a supportive friend, until you feel comfortable with the responses. Only then will you be ready to jump out into the real world and experience the assertive you.

Next, we will work on your negative self-talk. It is important that you refrain from putting yourself down. You will meet enough people willing to do that for you! Instead, start focusing on what you can do and not what you think you cannot do.

As the new assertive you begins to emerge, remember to keep your emotions in check. Being emotional will not help you in staying in control. You must remain calm at all times, especially if you want to be taken seriously in your encounters.

How do you do this? Realize that you have absolute control over your reactions. You can change and re-learn your reactions over your emotions. Let us try one exercise. This can help you relax before a stressful meeting.

Exercise:

Imagine yourself in a happy and comfortable place. *Others have imagined themselves in a Zen-like garden, a room that evokes a soothing atmosphere, in an open field, or in a nature scene.*

Breathe in deeply and begin to see yourself as part of the whole environment.

Exhale as you bask in the beauty of your surroundings.

Breathe in through the nose and then exhale slowly through the mouth. Do this breathing exercise three times.

You can also include meditation if you have sufficient time to enjoy the lasting effect. Or just relax listening to some soothing music.

If you have been staying at home for too long or have limited contact with a variety of people, dealing with the outside world can sometimes be daunting. Career professionals may make you feel inferior, ignorant, or less than adequate. You can overcome these feelings with a little preparation.

Preparation is the key. The more prepared you are, the more in control you will feel, and the more confident you will be.

Preparation means being aware of the particular situation that needs attention, knowing the person you need to talk to, and having a clear understanding of the message that you want to communicate. Writing it down will help ensure you cover every aspect and not miss a thing. Having it on paper in front of you will help keep you focused on the issue and minimize confusion and flustered feelings. It will also help if you will try to anticipate any responses or objections and plan how to address these concerns.

Part of the preparation is your overall projection. As unrelated and trivial as it may seem at first, you have to plan what you are going to wear.

Make sure it is something comfortable and appropriate for the occasion. They say that clothes do not make the person. However, knowing that you are dressed nicely and you look and feel good will give you more confidence.

Keep in mind that you do not need to justify every opinion or statement that you may make. Never apologize for being yourself. Some people can easily sense if you try to mask the real you. This is a major turn-off for the majority of people.

Exercise:

Okay, so you have written everything down and the basic script is ready and you are dressed to the "nines". It is now time for a little dress rehearsal.

Stand in front of a long mirror so you can see yourself clearly from head to toe.

While in front of the mirror, practice your body language. Stand straight. If this encounter is going to be in an office and you will be seated, pull a chair over to the mirror and practice how to gracefully sit down.

Look straight ahead and smile. Practice maintaining eye contact and looking alert and interested. Do not frown, for you do not want to appear angry and instead you want to project a calm and quiet confidence. You want to look determined, not daunting.

Watch your posture and remember to use easy gestures with your hands. Keep your voice intonation smooth and even. It is okay to sound determined, just do not overdo it too much. You should be passionate about the subject, but not emotional.

No matter how passionate you feel about the subject, keep your emotions in check all throughout the conversation. Negative emotions, such as anger, will only muddle the message that you are trying to communicate. The other party will end up confused and focused on your anger thereby not granting your request, whatever it is.

Make sure you have the right timing for setting up a meeting.

Everyone should be relaxed and hopefully, no one will be in a bad mood. Now practice what you are going to say in this encounter.

Remember to use assertive language -- that is, use clear and powerful words. Assertiveness counselors call these the "I" statements. Examples of this type of statements are: I think... I feel... I want... The way I see it... In my opinion... What I need is...

You will discover that individuals generally behave in one of three ways:

Non-assertive

A distinct trait of these people is they automatically withdraw from an encounter. They deny their feelings only to wind up allowing others to make decisions for them, then feel guilty or resentful when it happens. They let themselves be trapped into doing things they do not want to do or go where they do not want to go. Later on, they get angry with themselves and the ones who led them into the trap.

They are good at putting themselves down. Even their language is non-assertive:

It doesn't matter
Oh, that's okay
I didn't have a very good plan anyway, I'm sure yours is better.

Aggressive

These people have the tendency to overreact quickly to just about everything and are highly emotional. They tend to be domineering and controlling. If you will allow them, they would make decisions for you. They get hostile and defensive, making others feel hurt and humiliated. They will even resort to name calling, blaming, insults and sarcasm.

Their language reflects their aggressiveness:

We'll do it my way
I don't need to hear any more from you.
You don't even know what you're talking about!

Assertive

These people are the most open and direct. They are usually good communicators and negotiators. It is no wonder that compromise comes easily to them. They are able to view both sides of a situation, but they won't be made into doormats. They know what they want and they are not shy about letting you know. They are all about getting what they need and protecting their rights, but without stomping all over the other person's feelings and rights.

As you can see, assertive behavior and responses allow you to get your point across to the person, get what you need, and negotiate a good deal for yourself. You do not ever need to suffer through a hurtful relationship, attack someone else's self-esteem, or make someone defensive in any way. You can even persuade difficult people more easily by remaining calm, laying out your points and reasons, and acknowledging their side as well.

As you stand in front of a mirror, practice what you want to say and anticipate probable responses based on the type of person that you will be dealing with. Practice will make you feel more comfortable and confident when you approach the person in a real meeting.

When you feel you are prepared, walk out of that comfort zone. Be confident in meeting that important person and proceed to assert everything you have learned. Make sure you look sharp, stand up straight, shake his hand, and smile. Take a deep breath and start making your points.

Speak slowly and clearly. Do not mumble and dash through your prepared script.

Your notes are just there to keep you focused and to help you remember important points. Do not just read it; let it be your guide to what you want to say.

Listen and graciously allow the other person to respond now and then. He may want to discuss certain points and negotiate with you about your needs. Hopefully, you will reach an agreement at the end of the meeting. If this is not the case, allow him time to think. He may need to consider all you have said before making a final decision. It is okay to give him time to think. Pushing him to make a snap decision could work against you.

If it goes as well as you had hoped, you will feel a sense of elation and excitement. If you achieved your goal, you should definitely celebrate. You stepped outside of your comfort zone and did something you have never done before. Pat yourself on the back for a job well done. Your confidence level just jumped several points and you probably feel like you could take on the world.

When another time comes, allowing you to jump out of the comfort zone and display your newly acquired skills of confidence and assertiveness, remember this day and remind yourself, *"I did it before and I can do it again."* The first time is always the most difficult and each succeeding time will get easier and easier. Just keep practicing this very simple process and it will eventually become a habit that helps you get more of what you want more of the time.

Assertiveness in Times of Conflict

Another example of using assertiveness effectively is in the area of conflict and problem-solving. This often happens in the office, since you are dealing with so many diverse personalities. There is bound to be some conflict at one time or another.

This section can help you recognize the problem and resolve it peacefully and fairly. There are certain steps you must follow to successfully resolve a conflict with another co-worker.

If you have a problem with a co-worker, you should take it first to them in the hope of having a quick resolution. The problem could be as simple as a misunderstanding and a private chat could clear things up immediately.

Whatever you do, speak with that person privately; never criticize them in public. Always praise in public and condemn in private. However, humiliation will not help your cause. Speaking in private allows the other person to save face, especially if it is just a simple misunderstanding. The rest of the office need not know anything about it and you can lay it to rest quickly and with finality.

Try to speak to the person as soon as you encounter the problem. Problems left on their own and unresolved just grow bigger and bigger in the imagination. Go for a resolution as soon as you can.

Keep calm as you speak to the person and avoid getting defensive. At the same time, do not apologize for the issue you want to complain about.

Stick to the one issue that is bothering you. Do not begin by complaining that they always do something that is irritating or they never do something you think they should do. Focus on the complaint and do not deviate from that issue. The trick is to stick to 'The' Point and don't try and make 'A' Point.

Before you decide to speak to the person about that complaint, ask yourself if it is something that can be changed. The saying goes, "Change the changeable, accept the unchangeable, and avoid the unacceptable." Pick your battles. If it is a lost cause, move on. It is not worth beating your head against a brick wall.

Start by complimenting the person for something that he or she has accomplished in the past. Keep in mind that no one likes criticism. He will be more likely to step forward and solve the problem if you show that you appreciate his hard work in other areas.

If it appears that you have a hand in the conflict, own up to it, and become a part of the resolution as well. This will do a lot towards cementing relations in a large office. Always take the high road; do the right thing. Compromise does not mean you are not being assertive, it just means you know how to play fair.

Assertiveness in Dealing with Negative People

Assertiveness will also help you deal with the people who may constantly put you down. Instead of dealing with a problem and coming up with a resolution, they opt to insult and hurt your feelings.

Jules Feiffer calls these situations *"little murders"* as these are intended to insult, humiliate or embarrass others.

These people attack your self-confidence and your self-esteem. In the process, they *"murder"* what you have worked on so hard. Most of us just put up with these humiliating little put-downs, but that only encourages them. We learned earlier that we teach people how to treat us, so we need to teach them that these "little murders" are painful, humiliating, and need to be stopped. C. H. Spurgeon said, *"Insults are like bad coins; we cannot help their being offered us, but we need not take them."*

Sometimes the only way to avoid these put-downs is to avoid those delivering them. Remove yourself from their presence. Assert yourself and tell them it is unacceptable behavior, then leave. The barbs only work if you react and show them how upset you are.

Speak your mind, then leave. It leaves them with nothing; you have taken the wind from their sails. Eventually, they will learn that you cannot be drawn into their little insults any longer and they will lose interest in you.

So, you have learned how to:

- Grow more assertive, and not more aggressive.

- Adjust your behavior to get what you really, really want.

- Protect yourself and your individual rights.

- Say 'no' and not feel guilty afterward; you can cure this *disease to please*.

- Be respected for your actions and decisions.

- Bring up assertive children and teach them to be strong.

- Teach people how to treat you.

What is left for you to do now is simply to practice, practice, practice! Build up your self-confidence and self-esteem. You will become more likable and more self-accepting and confident in the process. It's a very simple exercise to follow through on and can result in a completely new you and a better life.

Use your mistakes to your advantage. They will teach you wisdom. *"Good judgment comes from experience, and often experience comes from bad judgment,"* said Rita Mae Brown.

Put all the knowledge and wisdom you have gained so far into your everyday life and see what happens. Still unconvinced of the benefits of asserting yourself?

Ask yourself, *"What's the worst thing that could happen to me if I learn to be assertive?"* Now ask yourself, *"What's the best thing that could happen to me if I learn to be assertive?"*

Imagine yourself in the position of really applying your newfound assertiveness. You have learned to stand up for yourself and people are no longer taking advantage of your good nature and willingness to help.

You have gained a brand-new position of authority at work doing only your own work. Your spouse has a newfound respect for you. Even your kids are more respectful since you taught them how to treat you. You are not being mean to anyone, just firm about how you intend to be treated from now on. Elbert Hubbard said, *"To know when to be generous and when to be firm -- that is wisdom."*

Remember, being assertive is about standing up for yourself and your rights, but without stomping on the other person's feelings and rights.

Your attitude, behavior, beliefs, and values are now in line with who you really are: an assertive, no-nonsense, action-oriented, take-charge kind of person!

Additional Information 1:

How to Assertively Ask for a Raise

One of the ways that assertiveness can help you is when it comes to asking for a raise. Almost everyone is nervous and unsure about how to approach the boss in this situation. Should you act humble or toot your own horn? Should you make an appointment with the boss or just try to corner him in a social atmosphere and send some hints?

Here again, is where the right sense of self-assertiveness comes in handy. You know that if you say nothing, nothing is probably what you will get. That yearly review will net you very little if you do not assert yourself now. Here are some guidelines for handling this sticky situation. Each boss or supervisor is different and so may require some adjustments.

Before you approach your boss or set up a time to meet with him, crunch a few numbers and decide how much money you need for that raise. Each company is different, but most will consider a raise of a certain percentage each year to cover the cost of living increases. In order to receive more than that, you have to be a stupendous worker, with an awesome background and have a penchant for making money for the company, to be of value and increase that value to the company wherever possible. The more productive and valuable you are, the better your chances for that raise.

Never pop in on your boss or supervisor with a request of this magnitude. You have to set aside time for this.

Just dropping in and making the request is unprofessional and rude. It would be inappropriate if you just break into his busy day asking for money. If you irritate your boss, your answer will be a swift and certain *"no"*.

Always make an appointment to speak with him and allow enough time so you would not feel rushed.

Make sure that you both sit down for this appointment. Sitting comfortably is more conducive for this kind of meeting. Standing around an office makes it too easy for the conversation to be interrupted, and there goes your chance to talk seriously about that raise you need and deserve.

Do not waste time with chitchat. Your boss or supervisor is a busy person and so are you. This is not a social visit; so, get right to your point. It may seem better and subtler to slowly introduce your concern into the conversation; but in reality, you are hurting your case by not getting to the point right away. He will respect you more if you get right to the main issue.

Make sure you have your script ready or at least some notes on what exactly you want to say. Go through the previous exercise to prepare for this meeting.

Nothing says unprofessional like hemming, hawing, and then not getting to the point. So, write down everything you want to say and focus on your goal -- make them realize why giving you a raise is in their best interest and the companies as well. Make certain you have rock solid reasons for the extra money.

A word of caution too - do not, I repeat, do not discuss this issue with anyone else in the office. The walls have ears and the last thing you need is for your request for a raise to reach your boss's office before you do. It looks unprofessional and indeed sneaky. In office politics, it is best for all involved if you do not talk about this meeting with anyone either before or after the meeting.

Just because the meeting went well, you do not have the reason to assume you are getting the raise and for you to start spreading the word all over the office. Your boss will not appreciate it and it could seriously hurt your chances.

Do not expect your boss to give you an answer right away. He has figures to check and probably has to discuss it with the Human Resource Department before making any decisions. Even your boss has to be accountable to higher-ups too, you know. If he requests for another meeting, be sure to have extra information that could aid your cause.

When your boss does call you in for a second meeting, listen carefully to what he has to say. Even if the answer to your original question of a raise turns out to be *"no"*, that does not mean it is the end of it. Be a good listener and ask questions when he is finished.

If he does not bring it up, ask why you did not qualify for a raise and do it politely. Getting angry and demanding concrete answers will not help you at all. Take a deep breath and calmly ask your boss what he recommends that you should do to increase your chances the next time. Find out how you can improve your performance. Be willing to do what is necessary (within reason, that is) to ensure that the next time you ask for a raise, you will receive a favorable reply.

Like it or not, the reward and punishment system is a fact of life. Objections to the system are a waste of time since everyone uses it. Take to heart what your boss tells you about improving your performance and put it into practice as soon as possible. Your willingness to improve weighs in your favor.

In the meantime, work on your self-confidence. Each task you do and accomplish adds to your self-confidence. Also, work on your negative self-talk. You are what you believe you are. Cultivate the habit to constantly think assertively, act assertively, and you will become assertive. Learning to be assertive at work will earn you the respect from your peers and your bosses. This might even increase your chances of getting a promotion and a raise in pay. Being assertive means speaking up for yourself, handling conflicts, and getting problems solved.

Additional Information 2:

Questions and Answers

Q: *What if I do become more assertive and I use what I have learned in my relationships, in my office work, or with friends; I even learned to say "no". What if people get angry with me?*

A: People who are truly your friends are not going to get mad at you. Real friends want you to learn and grow as a person. They will probably be happy for you now that you have learned to stop being a doormat. True friends want the best for you; in fact, they may have been secretly worried about you being such a pushover.

As for your spouse, if your partner truly loves you and wants the best for you, he/she will rejoice that you are learning to be more assertive and growing as a person. Your spouse's own life will be enriched by your experience. You will be more self-confident and happier, thereby making both of your lives better.

If you apply these skills to your job, your boss and co-workers will have more respect for you. At work, it can even mean getting a promotion, being assigned new and interesting challenges, or maybe even a raise. When your boss sees your capability to take control, handle crises, remain calm, and maintain poise, he will begin to see you in a completely new light.

Standing up for yourself makes a huge difference in the way people look at you and in how they treat you, especially at the office. It may be true that you cannot please everyone with your newly acquired skill. The ones who will not like the new you are probably the ones who used to push you around and may have taken advantage of you at every turn. Do not worry; they will get over it.

Stop depriving yourself of the respect due to you. Be assertive and earn other people's respect. Be in control of your life and feel more self-confident. Your life will never be the same again.

Q: *If others do get angry with me, how do I handle it? What if I fall apart?*

A: If you use these new skills appropriately, things will change, situations will improve and yes, you will earn the anger of some people. As previously pointed out, those who will get angry are probably the ones who used to mistreat you. However, you are improving your own life and protecting your rights. They are upset because they can no longer push you around, infringe on your personal rights, and pass on to you the jobs they do not wish to do.

That is the reason why they are angry. Bear in mind that you are not responsible for their feelings. They will have to deal with their own feelings. It is now their problem, not yours.

Q: *Are my friends going to get mad when I start telling them "no" all the time?*

A: They would be more upset to know that you have been saying *"yes"* to everyone when you really mean to say *"no"*. Agreeing to things that you really do not want to do will begin to make you feel resentful towards that person. You hate feeling that way towards your close friends, right? It is almost as if you have been lying to them.

Being assertive and saying *"no"* is a more honest approach, don't you think? Or would you rather risk destroying their love and respect just because you cannot say *"no"*?

Q: *What about saying "no" at work; won't that get me in trouble?*

A: By agreeing to everything that everyone wants you to do at work, you will find that you simply cannot keep up with all the work. There are just so many hours in a day. If you say *"yes"* to everything, you are cheating yourself and the others who are depending on you to finish what you said you would do.

Doing shoddy work is not going to impress anyone. By taking on too much, you would not have the time to do a good job on everything. By limiting the number of jobs, you accept, you are actually doing everyone and the company a favor. If you keep the workload down, you can do a great job on your assignments. This is what will impress people. It is better to cut the workload and finish everything well than to take on too much and then to finish nothing.

Q: *What if someone asks me to do something I know I can easily accomplish and yet, I say "no"; will he think that I'm selfish or self-centered?*

A: Just because you can do something does not mean you have to do it. You can refuse even legitimate requests assertively so long as they aren't tasks you were employed to complete in the first place. Sometimes, you have to put your own needs ahead of others. You cannot please everyone all the time and you do not have to. Bitterness will grow if you let the guilt get to you and make you a *'yes'* person all the time.

Q: *If I'm assertive about what I know and what I can do, won't that make me sound egocentric? Shouldn't I be more modest?*

A: Being assertive and letting people know you are clever and skilled is not being immodest or egocentric. Sometimes you have to toot your own horn, so to speak, and there is nothing wrong with that. If you do not do it, who will? Sometimes being modest is not a very good option. It makes you sound like you cannot say anything positive about yourself. It also indicates that you cannot give or receive compliments.

Q: *If I toot my own horn, as you say, won't people expect me to be great 100% of the time? What if I screw up?*

A: Without being assertive and letting others know of your skills and accomplishments, you will miss out on many opportunities. Since no one is perfect, you will make mistakes occasionally. Own up to them and learn from them, then move on.

Even if you mess up once in a while, you will be respected far more for giving it your best shot than by not trying at all. As Wayne Gretzky, the hockey player said, *"You'll always miss 100% of the shots you don't take."*

Q: *I'm a woman and I'm not sure it's considered feminine to be assertive all the time. Men can get away with it, but not women. Will men in my office hate me if I try to be more assertive in the workplace?*

A: It is unfortunate that assertive women often have more trouble at work than their male counterparts. However, that should not stop any woman from standing up for herself in the workplace. If you possess the skills necessary for the job and have all of the experience and drive, you can assert yourself and get what you want.

A woman in a management position may find herself walking in a fine line. She must be assertive in order to do her job but may be thought of as pushy or unfeminine when she does. Oddly enough, studies done on this topic showed that the criticism came mostly from other women, not the men in the workplace.

Someone once said that we should learn to live without the good opinions of others. If your career is important to you, you will have to learn to be assertive and be selective about considering other people's opinions.

Thanks for Listening

Did You Enjoy Reading Your Assertive Life?

I would like to thank you for purchasing and reading this book. I hope you enjoyed it and that it provided some value to yourself and your life.

If you enjoyed reading this book and found some benefit in it, I'd love your support and hope that you could take a moment to post a review. I'd love to hear from you, even if you have feedback, as it will help me in ensuring that I improve this book and others in the future.

To leave your review I have made it as easy as possible for you. Just visit or click your preffered link below.

Click Here To Leave Your Review *(United States)*
https://www.amazon.com/dp/1913929299

Other Books by Andy Raingold

Attitude Advantage
Freedom from Addictions
Your Assertive Life
Attraction Master
Communication Master
Focused Concentration
Fast Learning Genius
Enhance Yourself and Your Life
Unlimited Energy
Set High Goals Then Reach Them
Reboot Your Metabolism
Mind Mapping Mastery Tips
Raise Your Motivational Power
Easily Defeat & Dump Procrastination
Subconscious Programming
Tap into The Universe
Unleash Your Power
Creative Visualization
Your Perfect Memory
Your Unlimited Power
Strategies to Boost Productivity
How to Become an Effective Manifestor
Boost Your Self Esteem
Listen to Yourself

Free Books

First Level VIP: Mastering Your Destiny *(www.firstlevel.vip)*
Second Level VIP: Your Seven Step Goal Setting Workshop
Third Level VIP: 5 Ways to Develop A Mindset for Success

(www.firstlevel.vip)
(www.secondlevel.vip)
(www.thirdlevel.vip)

The above three levels of success each contain:

- **An initial free product.**
    - Mastering Your Destiny
    - Your Seven Step Goal Setting Workshop
    - 5 Ways to Develop A Mindset for Success
- **A Success Letter.**
- **Main Product/Subject Area.**
    - The Better Life Experience Program
    - Super Productive Power Funnels Program
    - Creating Your Own Universe Program

Each deal with a specific subject:

First Level: Knowing what you want. **LIFE PURPOSE**
Second Level: Knowing how to get there. **SETTING GOALS**
Third Level: Knowing how to act on the way there. **MINDSET**

DISCLAIMER AND TERMS OF USE AGREEMENT

The author and publisher have used their best efforts in preparing this report. The author and publisher make no representation or warranties with respect to the accuracy, applicability, fitness, or completeness of the contents of this report. The information contained in this report is strictly for educational purposes. Therefore, if you wish to apply ideas contained in this report, you are taking full responsibility for your actions.

EVERY EFFORT HAS BEEN MADE TO ACCURATELY REPRESENT THIS PRODUCT AND Its POTENTIAL. HOWEVER, THERE IS NO GUARANTEE THAT YOU WILL IMPROVE IN ANY WAY USING THE TECHNIQUES AND IDEAS IN THESE MATERIALS. EXAMPLES IN THESE MATERIALS ARE NOT TO BE INTERPRETED AS A PROMISE OR GUARANTEE OF ANYTHING. SELF-HELP AND IMPROVEMENT POTENTIAL IS ENTIRELY DEPENDENT ON THE PERSON USING OUR PRODUCT, IDEAS AND TECHNIQUES.

YOUR LEVEL OF IMPROVEMENT IN ATTAINING THE RESULTS CLAIMED IN OUR MATERIALS DEPENDS ON THE TIME YOU DEVOTE TO THE PROGRAM, IDEAS AND TECHNIQUES MENTIONED, KNOWLEDGE AND VARIOUS SKILLS. SINCE THESE FACTORS DIFFER ACCORDING TO INDIVIDUALS, WE CANNOT GUARANTEE YOUR SUCCESS OR IMPROVEMENT LEVEL. NOR ARE WE RESPONSIBLE FOR ANY OF YOUR ACTIONS.

MANY FACTORS WILL BE IMPORTANT IN DETERMINING YOUR ACTUAL RESULTS AND NO GUARANTEES ARE MADE THAT YOU WILL ACHIEVE RESULTS SIMILAR TO OURS OR ANYBODY ELSE'S, IN FACT NO GUARANTEES ARE MADE THAT YOU WILL ACHIEVE ANY RESULTS FROM OUR IDEAS AND TECHNIQUES IN OUR MATERIAL.

The author and publisher disclaim any warranties (express or implied), merchantability, or fitness for any particular purpose. The author and publisher shall in no event be held liable to any party for any direct, indirect, punitive, special, incidental or other consequential damages arising directly or indirectly from any use of this material, which is provided "as is", and without warranties.

As always, the advice of a competent professional should be sought.

The author and publisher do not warrant the performance, effectiveness or applicability of any sites listed or linked to in this book. All links are for information purposes only and are not warranted for content, accuracy or any other implied or explicit purpose.

www.ingramcontent.com/pod-product-compliance
Lightning Source LLC
Chambersburg PA
CBHW071536080526
44588CB00011B/1683